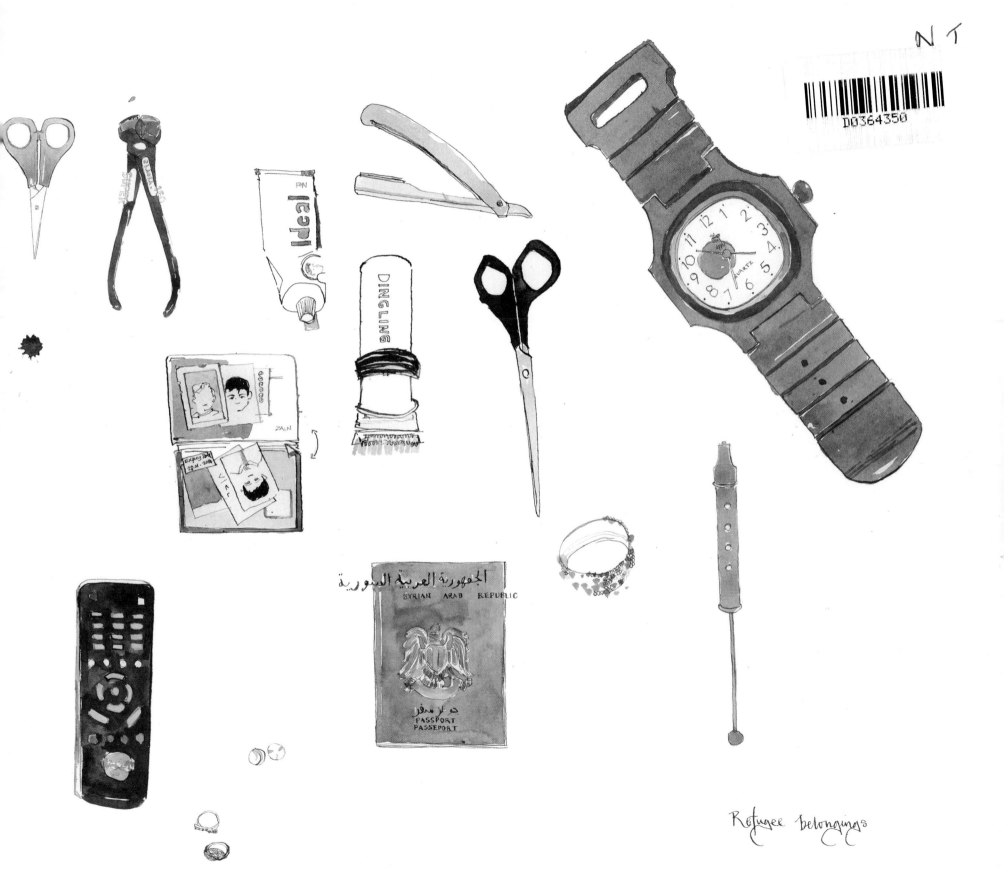

Refugee belongings

With thanks to Emily Miller from the Migration Museum, London

Some names have been changed to protect individuals' anonymity.

First published 2021 by Walker Studio, an imprint of Walker Books Ltd, 87 Vauxhall Walk, London SE11 5HJ

1 2 3 4 5 6 7 8 9 10

© 2021 George Butler

The right of George Butler to be identified as author/illustrator of this work has been asserted by him
in accordance with the Copyright, Designs and Patents Act 1988

This book has been typeset in Helvetica Neue

Printed in China

British Library Cataloguing in Publication Data: a catalogue record for this book is available from the British Library

ISBN 978-1-4063-9216-6

www.walkerstudio.com

DRAWN ACROSS BORDERS
TRUE STORIES OF MIGRATION

WALKER STUDIO
AN IMPRINT OF WALKER BOOKS

Abdullo *Farouk* *Abdul* *Abed* *Hasan* *Zouhair*

CONTENTS

Hani *Guram* *Farid* *Ahmed* *Yusef* *Mustafa*

Karam

Hadi

Abbas

Manfri

Hamza

Ibrahim

INTRODUCTION

It is an unusual feeling to walk into a place that everyone is leaving. I have been stared at as if I am lost or mad, and sometimes I have felt as if I'm both. However, by resisting the temptation to turn around and walk away I have made these drawings. I made them in refugee camps, war zones and on the move, and as I drew, people told me their stories.

I was often only able to spend a short time with these people, but they displayed such humanity and such generosity of spirit, that for that moment they eclipsed the traumas and pressures that were forcing them to migrate.

People move around the world for many reasons. Some migration is voluntary; most is not. People move for love, work, security, war, food and family. They have done so for hundreds of thousands of years and they still do. It runs deep in the human condition, but is an intricate, sprawling subject for anyone to comprehend.

We live in an increasingly interconnected world but run the risk of having a far shallower understanding of the individuals in it. I hope this book can offer a glimpse into some of the reasons people have for leaving behind places they once called home, places that many still call home.

What is clear to me as we begin a new decade – as the population increases, resources remain limited and climate pressures mount – is that migration will vastly alter the future of the world and our species. Only by understanding individual cases better can we properly respond to migration as a whole.

I'm grateful to the people who sat still for long enough to be drawn, but even more appreciative of the time and energy it takes to tell a personal story, having tried it myself. I hope the images do the honesty of their words justice.

George Butler

Leila

Mama Nazak

Jeelan

Khalid

Karam

Ezat

Syria

ARRIVING IN A PLACE EVERYONE ELSE IS LEAVING

In March 2011, following peaceful demonstrations against the government, a civil war erupted in Syria and flared quickly into a bloody conflict. Many militias were fighting for different reasons, and all sides were capable of acts of extreme violence, in particular the government of Bashar al-Assad. The civilian casualties were rising faster than they could be counted.

A year later, in August 2012, I walked across the border from Turkey into Syria expecting to find an exodus of people trying to get away. But the border was empty. So empty I had to search for officials to stamp my passport.

I was picked up by the Free Syrian Army and driven past bullet-ridden buildings, olive groves damaged by tanks and a petrol station caught in crossfire. We soon arrived at Azaz, a town in northern Syria. Muhammad, my translator and an English student from Aleppo University, explained how thousands of people had fled this small town when the fighting broke out. Most people moved to family homes in the countryside, not expecting the shelling to last. Few believed they would have to leave the country.

Later that day in the town square I drew children playing on a burnt-out government tank as two old men examined the total destruction of their town in bewilderment. Their homes would continue to be the targets of government air strikes for years to come.

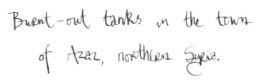

Burnt-out tanks in the town of Azaz, northern Syria.

I wandered through the town with Muhammad and saw the bakery. I had to draw quickly because of the pounding Syrian sun. People queued in this heat for up to three hours and, as Muhammad explained, each person was only allowed three pieces of flatbread a day.

Queuing for the bakery

Azaz prison

That evening a member of the Free Syrian Army called Firas took me to visit one of their prisons in Azaz. One man behind the bars looked at me intimidatingly. I assumed he was cross that I was drawing him. He held my gaze, unflinching, as I drew. Then after fifteen minutes or so he asked if he could move. All along he had been posing for the strange illustrator.

It wasn't until I was leaving Syria that I found the migration I had expected from the start. At the border I began to draw a car with a family inside, but the father insisted on standing in the way, as if to protect his family from me. As soon as I explained what I was doing, he happily let the drawing continue, telling me that he was all packed up and taking his family away. He didn't know where to.

A family at the Syrian border.

Tajikistan

MIGRATING TO FIND WORK

When the Soviet Union collapsed in 1991, the newly independent Tajikistan was left poor and without resources. Since then, many of its people have relied on taking the train that leaves Dushanbe, the capital, twice a week and finding work in Russia. On its four-day journey the train winds its way through Uzbekistan, Turkmenistan, Kazakhstan and into Moscow. What little money people make there they send home. When I visited Tajikistan in 2015, an estimated 50 per cent of the economy was supported in this way.

I followed Abdullo, a young Tajik man whose father had been killed in the civil war that started after the country gained independence, to catch the train to Moscow. This was his fourth trip to Russia. Each time he stayed for six months, working on freezing construction sites, and sent the money he earned back to his mother, wife and baby daughter in the Rasht Valley.

Abdullo told me how hard it was to leave his friends and family. "When I was younger I didn't study because we had no money, the situation was ugly… I first went to Russia in 2008, back then it was easy," he said. "My friends are working there in Russia, but their thoughts are here [in Tajikistan], that their families are not hungry – the money they depend on all comes from Moscow."

The conditions on the train were atrocious and I could see the ways in which Tajiks were treated as second-class citizens, as the train guards searched my bags, asked aggressive questions and even suggested I was a spy.

Packed train from Dushanbe to Moscow

Abdullo

When I first met Abdullo he had been a confident figure with his bright pink T-shirt, cowboy hat and a cigarette hanging from his bottom lip. As we got closer to Moscow I observed his body language change: his shoulders became hunched, he smoked more and pulled his hood low over his eyes. His discomfort was obvious.

Tajik migrants work in twos and threes to renovate the interiors of some of the new apartment buildings being built across Moscow. At night, workspace becomes living space. Many migrants choose not to leave the sites at all, spending months in one apartment after another, rather than risk attracting attention from the police. It struck me that human migration is often thought of as one-directional, but this movement of people is on a continuous loop – an enormous, annual commute to work.

Building site in Moscow

Not everyone can make this long journey. I returned to Tajikistan to speak to those left behind. One morning in the rural Rasht Valley, I followed a young boy called Abdul Kareem as he set off from his village with his herd of goats, straight up a mountain. As I caught my breath and began to draw him, he told me, "My father has worked in Moscow for one and a half years, only returning when he fell ill. I want to go to Russia to work in construction too … or just to go with my father. I miss him when he is there."

I forgot during this grown-up conversation about life that Abdul was only twelve. And no sooner had I started my drawing than he stood up and ran back down the mountain for school in the afternoon. As he left he said, "I like English the most because if you can read it you can speak it."

Abdul tending his goats
in the Rasht Valley

I spent a rainy day in Dushanbe drawing the men who wait on the street to be employed locally. They carry their tools with them to show their trade and leave them on the street with a "Call me" note. If that particular tool fits the job, customers will call. It's a precarious living for those who can't travel to find work elsewhere.

Waiting for work in Dushanbe

Myanmar

THE MODERN-DAY NOMAD

The terrible plight of the Rohingya people in Myanmar is now well known all over the world. When I first visited the country in 2013 the most recent crisis had not yet been widely reported, and I was not permitted to enter the camps where the Rohingya now lived. Instead I was directed to draw in the camps of the Arakanese people. They are people from Rakhine State and a Myanmar ethnic group that had been internally displaced from the recent fighting between them and the Rohingya.

While many people were forced to move around Myanmar to flee persecution, others migrated to support the country's trade, and so when I returned to Myanmar in 2015 and was still not allowed to visit the Rohingya camps, this is what I decided to investigate instead.

I took the overnight bus to Magwe, central Myanmar, hired a motorbike and drove slowly 100 kilometres south through the farms and paddy fields, every so often crossing a wooden bridge being rebuilt in concrete to withstand the annual monsoon.

Eventually I reached a mass of blue and green tarpaulin tents, strung up amongst posts and wires in the bottom of a valley. As I got closer the churning noise of generators became louder than the motorbike. Under each tarpaulin I found a team of two or three people digging and pumping out crude oil.

Camp for displaced
Arakanese people, Myanmar.

I spoke to U Win and Daw Aye Kyi, a couple who used to farm but have since started digging for oil. "Being a farmer cannot feed us enough but this business does," explained Daw Aye Kyi. "Initially we sold all our cows and buffalo for the $6,000 we needed to begin digging for oil. We used to farm sesame seeds – now we have had oil for three years."

Each day the oil brokers came in a truck from the nearby city of Monywa to take the oil away. At the time I was there U Win and Daw Aye Kyi were selling their oil for $70 a barrel, and could produce between two and ten barrels a day. This money was enough to significantly change the fortunes of their whole family. Once their plot ran dry they would pay the landowner to be allowed to dig another well near by.

In places like Myanmar migration is vital to reach the resources needed to survive. And so these modern nomads make their way slowly across the landscape, looking for new places to dig. It was, however, those who were not migrating out of choice – those who were fleeing for their lives – that drew international attention to the country.

Digging for crude oil

Two men working the pumps

The Balkan Route

NEW BORDERS BEING BUILT ACROSS EUROPE

In the summer of 2015 the "refugee crisis" in Europe became very visible in Greece, with people fleeing wars in Syria, Iraq and Afghanistan and others escaping persecution and violence in North and East Africa. Greece was one of the places where they could cross the border into Europe and find safety, before many continued either on foot or by train through the Balkan countries. I wanted to speak to people who were trying to make that journey, even as European governments started to block their path.

I visited Idomeni in northern Greece in December 2015, where on a nondescript, wet and muddy piece of railway line in the arable fields there was a tall, newly built fence. On one side armoured police patrolled with batons, while groups of refugees and migrants, carrying their lives and children on their backs, were on the other.

Several hundred metres away from the tension surrounding the fence were dozens of tents. It was there I spoke to fifteen-year-old Ahmed, who described his journey here: "Life in Iraq was fine until armed groups came. We left our homes — what else was there to do? We fled to the mountains. I stayed for eight days without food or water — nothing was there. Children died of hunger — nothing was there.

Tents set up by refugees in Idomeni, northern Greece.

Ahmed

"We crossed into Turkey on foot. It took us one to two days' walking. Yes, we were scared. We walked at night — and it was scary on the boat too. It was difficult — the sea waves were a metre or two high. We had children on the dinghy ... 150 people on the boat, honestly. We were on the boat for two hours at sea.

"We are going to Germany. We want to live a decent and simple life — that's it. Tonight? We have no idea where to sleep — in the tent or in the street — we don't know. We don't know where to go. We wanted to take the train but there were no tickets."

In the camp the following morning, as I was drawing, a small riot broke out as people scrambled up the back of a lorry to get their hands on much-needed food, bedding and medical supplies. Once order was restored the migrants and refugees queued, as they did each day, around the edge of the field. I vividly remember making this particular drawing because amongst all the cold, wrapped-up faces, a little girl in a brightly coloured hat watched me intently from the front of the queue. Whenever I caught her eye she smiled. It was a warm smile in a sad place. It's easy to remember those happier moments and those individuals, especially the children, but the trauma and severity of the crisis runs much deeper.

Queuing for food.

I left the camp and drove in the same direction many of these refugees were travelling, through the Balkan countries of Southeast Europe. In the town of Preševo in southern Serbia, I boarded a train and met Afghan refugees who'd made it this far after first arriving in Greece. They were waiting on the train hours before it was due to leave so they could stay out of the cold. Meanwhile, others on the railway platform were burning rubbish to keep warm. They were all tired from their journey here, but hoping they'd be allowed to continue into Western Europe.

In 2012 I had watched Syrians as they were forced to flee their homes to find peace, a decision no one could have argued with. And yet only thirty-six months later, those same people, along with those from Afghanistan, Iraq and elsewhere, were seeking refuge in Europe and often being turned away. I wondered how much further all the people I'd met would be able to travel before a European government stopped them.

Burning rubbish for warmth on the railway platform

On the train in Preševo, Serbia

Kenya

MOVING FROM RURAL LIFE TO THE CITY

Not all migration means leaving a country behind. Urbanization in developing countries means many people move to cities in search of work, education and security. In 2007, for the first time more than half the population of the world lived in cities. It is thought that the figure will be 66 per cent by 2050. In 2018 I visited Kenya to try to understand how people migrate in a country with a fast-growing population and a high proportion of people under twenty-five years old.

Two hours off the tarmac road near Amboseli, south Kenya, I met Kimoono. He was a Maasai herdsman and a Lion Guardian – a member of a community group who protect the local wildlife. Kimoono lived with his family and his herd of cows in a boma, a circle of small huts surrounded by thorn bushes to keep his animals in and other animals out. The Maasai existence is intrinsically connected to migration. Throughout history they have lived nomadically, moving great distances with their livestock. Although Kimoono would think nothing of walking 20 or 30 or 40 kilometres with his cattle to graze or find water, now he rarely moves his boma where he lives with his mother, brothers, their wives and children.

Kimoono, a Maasai herdsman, with his cattle

It is easy to romanticize rural Kenyan life, but the reality is that an increasing number of people are moving to cities in search of a better alternative. Many arrive at the Machakos Country Bus Station in Nairobi. It was impossible to capture all the intense activity there on a single sheet of paper. On my left were buses covered in vibrant graffiti framing the faces of passengers sitting at each window. On my right, busy and excited groups of men in uniforms that matched the colour of their buses loaded the roof racks with sofas, motorbikes and vegetables.

Machakos Country Bus Station, Nairobi

I moved on to Kibera, one of the infamous slums in Nairobi. This settlement of informal homes has grown over the last fifty years as many people have arrived in the city with the hope of finding work. As I drew a group of children skipping, a man leant over my shoulder and watched. I held a pen, he held a hammer. Jossy had moved to Kibera in the 1980s in search of work. As we chatted he explained, "I was looking for any job lifting things." From his build I could see why. We talked about football and how more people in England watched football than went to church. "Do you know Wayne Rooney?" he asked. "Tell Wayne to go to church." He was quite cross when I suggested I might not be able to.

At the top of the hill is the railway line used as a footpath from one side of the slums to the other. Again I had a voice in my ear. Sami was fourteen, spoke fluent English and told me that he wanted to come to England to play football and go to university. "I have a talent – how should I do it?" To prove his ambition and his ability, he said he could name any capital city in the world. I tested him, and he could … and for good measure he listed the British Prime Ministers too.

We talked about school and university and Sami asked, "Could you take me with you?" It's the question I dread but I know is always coming. The answer is no – the practicalities make it almost impossible. But I find it so hard to say. Sami had the same ambition as so many young people I have met all over the world. I just hoped he'd have the opportunity to fulfil it.

A street in Kibera, Nairobi

Iraq

FAMILIES ESCAPING THE FRONT LINE

In April 2017, in the middle of the Old City in West Mosul, the Iraqi Army Golden Division were at the forefront of the world's fight against the radical militant group Daesh (also known as Islamic State or ISIS). The army had circled the Daesh stronghold and many local people were caught up in the fighting.

On my way to the front line, out of the pillar-box view of the Iraqi Army Humvee, I saw a family pushing their grandmother in a wheelbarrow. Dressed all in black, she waved at us as if this was normal, as you would from the top deck of a bus. Like many others they were fleeing the destroyed city and heading for the camps for those who were internally displaced.

Once I arrived on the front line in the Tanak district of West Mosul, I sat with Ahmed, a young soldier. We talked and he smoked shisha as he waited for leave. From the rooftop above it was his and his colleagues' job to guide in missiles to Daesh positions, destroying another building, another home, and displacing civilians.

The fighting caused chaos for the people who lived here. The roads in West Mosul were completely blocked, littered with burnt-out cars, or destroyed by tactical air strikes to stop Daesh movements, so many people were forced to leave on foot.

Al Nabi Street, Tanak district, West Mosul

And yet … in the middle of this migration some people were returning home as the fighting moved elsewhere. This wasn't a clearly defined front line, but people trying to live their lives around the fringes of atrocity.

Further away from the fighting, I met Abdul Hamid outside his house in West Mosul. He offered me a seat and, as was so often the case, I was handed a glass of sweet tea. I sat down to draw Abdul and his three friends clearing the rubble from his home. After a while he came over and told me what had happened a month earlier.

"On the 17th March [2017] four Daesh fighters came out of the 'new mosque' [south of al Thawra neighbourhood]. They were under fire from the Iraqi security forces and they ran into the nearest building, which was my house," he said. "The gunfight resumed for a short time until all went quiet. Fifteen minutes passed and an air strike was called in… Four missiles hit my home… The missiles killed the four Daesh fighters but they also killed my mother, two of my brothers and one of their wives." He paused. "We are here to see if anything is left," he said dismissively, gesturing at a mangled washing machine. The taxi they drove for a living was crushed under the rubble. "The government will provide help if you are willing to move to a camp, but they give nothing to those who stay in their homes."

Talking to Abdul, I saw so clearly how civilians suffer in war. They are left with little choice: either move to an unfriendly but slightly safer internal displacement camp, or stay at home, in the firing line.

Abdul Hamid's family home

Serbia

THE ROUTE TO EUROPE

The unlikely combination of snow and queues of refugees had attracted swathes of the world's photojournalists to Serbia, a country on the overground route for refugees from the Middle East to Europe. Many journalists, like me, had been following the story of Syrian, Iraqi and Afghan refugees fleeing their countries. However, in January 2017 Belgrade was also home to economic migrants – those who left home in search of work – from Pakistan, Bangladesh and North Africa.

Both refugees and migrants were stuck at borders all across Europe, as governments built walls and deployed police forces to control who was crossing them. In this dark place it was hard to differentiate between the reasons people had for travelling.

When I arrived in Belgrade, I was immediately struck by the cold. But there are two types of cold here: the cold you rush through from one building to another, as I was able to, and the cold you have to sit in. Refugees and migrants here had a different relationship to the cold. Everything they did was to combat it.

In a warehouse at the back of the Belgrade railway station, thousands of people huddled together in groups, burning railway sleepers, clothes and plastic to keep warm. In the evenings they stacked cardboard to lift themselves up off the concrete floor, which was below freezing all hours of the day. As I drew I could feel the cold soaking up into my boots. I'll never forget the smell of the burning plastic, the toxic fumes that filled the refugees' lungs – a necessary evil to keep them warm.

Refugees trying to keep warm in a warehouse in Belgrade

Most of the refugees and migrants there were men, especially from the Middle East, as they saw it as too dangerous a journey for their wives and daughters to make. Even in the afternoon sun I found them wrapped in blankets, as if they were so used to being cold at night they kept the blanket on all day even when it was unnecessary.

I spoke to Ezat, who was from Afghanistan. He had worked for the US Army as a translator in Kandahar in 2013. When the Americans left, the security risks increased for Ezat. He told me, "In the beginning of 2016, some groups of ISIS came to my village. After a while they started bothering the people in the village. I had a TV, they came into my house at 2 a.m. and took it... I had to pay 10,000 Afghani, which is like $150. Things were getting worse each day. I didn't feel safe because I had worked for the US Army, so my family told me to leave before anything happened to me. I asked them where did they want me to go? They said Europe."

It took Ezat one year to get to Serbia. He was attacked by Bulgarian police, beaten up, and had to pay $5,000 to a smuggler to be released from the cell he had been kept in. His family had sent the money.

Ezat

Queuing for soup.

Each morning in the railway siding I watched an old oil drum filled with water being slowly heated. By eleven it was warm enough to wash with and some of the migrants got undressed, balanced their clothes on dry stones above the snow and resisted the freezing temperatures to briefly feel the normality of washing again. Journalists, myself included, crowded round taking pictures of this vulnerable moment. In the distance I could see the hotels of Belgrade, I imagined with en suite showers in each room, and I felt helpless.

Elsewhere I saw people queuing for soup, or sitting in cafés as they tried to call home. One evening I spotted a little café in the park in the centre of Belgrade. I couldn't understand what was going on at first. Lots of people were gathered around plastic tables, but none of them were drinking anything. As I got closer I saw that on each table was a lifeline: a multi-socket adaptor on which migrants charged their phones, which were often their only connection to family at home and to smugglers. Without them the uncertainty of where they would go next would have surely been unbearable.

Charging phones in a café

FINDING KINDNESS IN UNEXPECTED PLACES

I'd come back to Syria in 2013 by invitation of a local organization delivering aid in Idlib, a city in the northwest of the country. The war was still raging and they felt there was an untold story about civilian suffering.

My first assignment was at a children's ward in a field hospital inside Syria, near the border with Turkey. War photographers often talk about hiding behind a camera and, on this day, I did the same behind my drawing board. I drew Bassam, who was ten. Three days earlier he had lost his brother, his mother and his left leg in an air strike. The nurse came in and pulled the blankets from Bassam's bed to reveal his injury. She said nothing but I knew what she was telling me – if you want to know what really happens here, look at this…

Bassam's father Abid sat at the foot of his bed, in black, occasionally putting a reassuring hand on his son's foot as he struggled through the painkillers. "Art cannot change anything," he said to me, and in this moment I believed him. My instinct was to leave without finishing the drawing. But another man in the corner said passionately, "These are the sorts of scenes that the world should see. They are important to show the people what is going on here." Perhaps it was these contradicting opinions that led to the unfinished nature of this picture.

500
600
700
800
900

Bassam and his father Abid in the children's
ward of the field hospital in Syria.

Several days later in the town of Taftanaz I stood at a crossroads, surrounded by buildings rearranged by war. I began to work – pen in one hand, pot of ink and paper in the other – when the noise of a tank firing split the air. I froze, ready to dive to the floor, but a group of locals next to me simply put their fingers in their ears. They were used to this. The projectile thudded somewhere in the distance and I pretended I was calm – although I was struggling to hold the page still.

Damaged buildings in Taftanaz, northwest Syria

Mama Nazak

Back in Turkey at a refugee camp in Kilis I met sixty-year-old Nazak Kurdi, known as Mama Nazak, a mother of three and a geography teacher, and twelve-year-old Ibrahim. They were both from Syria and they wanted to share their stories with me.

Although Mama Nazak told me a horrifying story of torture and great loss, I felt she was protecting me from her real agony. She said, "I am a geography teacher, but I was expelled from the university for not being a member of the Ba'ath Party… I was hung by one hand for twenty days, by the regime of Hafez al-Assad." She showed me the scarred flesh on her arm.

She and her husband fled to Egypt in the 1980s with their three boys, Firas, Faris and Jama. They returned to Syria but migrated to Turkey again when the war started in 2011. This time her sons returned to fight the regime. Mama Nazak begged them not to go. "Firas was killed in action… Faris had a tear in his stomach from shrapnel and Jama was shot in the hand."

Then she looked at me and said, "You can say I had three flowers in my garden. One was eaten by the beast and two were trampled down with the beast's foot as he walked away."

Ibrahim's story was no less horrific and yet he spoke so calmly. Both his parents were killed in front of him and he had fled his home in Syria. He told me, "When I grow up, I'd like to be a policeman so that if someone enters my house again I can protect my family. Or a doctor so I can heal the injured people of the war."

Mama Nazak had adopted Ibrahim in the refugee camp where they now lived. She said, "I feel everyone the age of my children is a son to me." It was this generosity of spirit in the midst of war that remained with me.

Ibrahim

Palestine

THE RIGHT TO MOVE

In 1947 the United Nations divided Palestine into an Arab state (Palestine) and a Jewish state (Israel). This led to one of the most controversial and unresolved conflicts of modern times. Opinion is still divided as to where the borders should lie and who owns the land, and over the years fighting has displaced hundreds of thousands of Palestinians. Many have had to flee their homes to refugee camps.

In Gaza, a strip of land that is part of Palestine and blockaded by Israel, there are refugee camps that were first set up in 1948, and which are still lived in seventy years later. I visited Gaza City in August 2016 with Kamal, a local taxi driver. He told me, "Gaza is one of the most populated places on earth. Jabalia [a refugee camp] has 114,000 people in a square mile." I had imagined the camp would be full of tents, but it was a breeze-block maze of poorly built homes. Kamal explained, "They are still called camps because no one owns the land."

My visit to the Gaza Strip was only allowed to last for twenty-four hours. Before I left I visited the town of Az-Zawayda to see what families from the nearby camps did during the day. On the beach I drew a group of women, accompanied by a young man, sitting watching their children paddling. I was struck by how familiar this scene would seem to families all over the world, although here it was taking place in the context of conflict.

Families from refugee camps on the beach near Az-Zawayda.

For Palestinians movement is heavily restricted, especially crossing the borders controlled by the Israeli and Egyptian authorities. This makes seeing family, getting to school, medical trips and work hard for a predominantly young population.

I travelled to the West Bank, another disputed area controlled by Israel where millions of Palestinians live. Down the road towards Jerusalem we found Umm al-Khair, a small village that had been demolished by Israeli forces the day before. Families stood around the remains of their homes and children played in the rubble. They were not as outwardly angry as I had expected, just quiet.

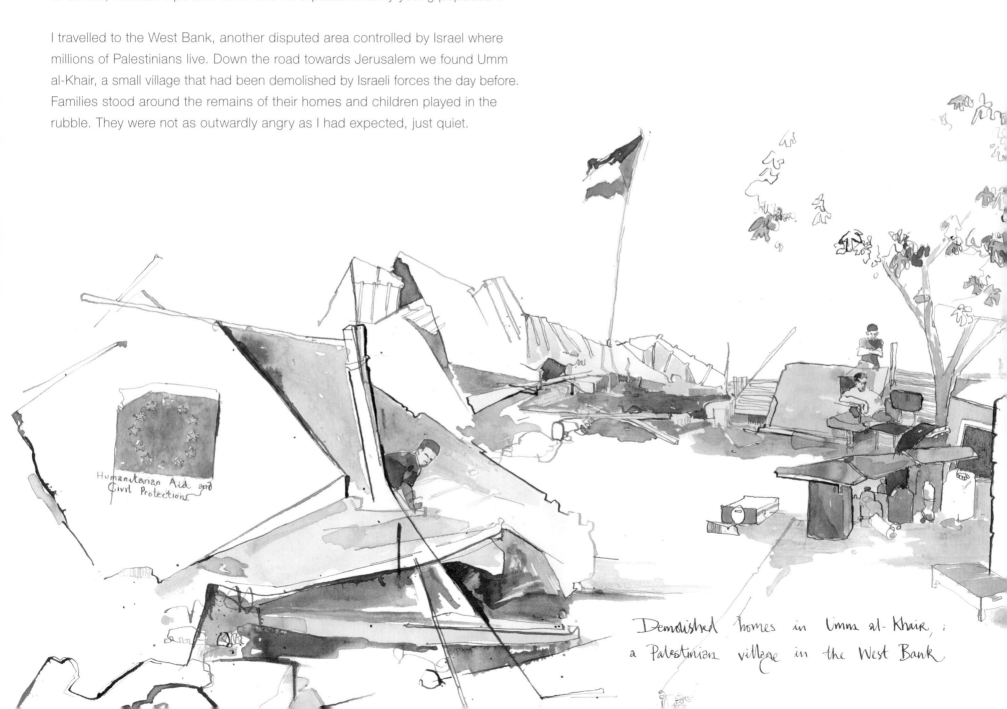

Humanitarian Aid and Civil Protection

Demolished homes in Umm al-Khair, a Palestinian village in the West Bank

The wall in Bethlehem, West Bank

Abbas

I continued on to the E1 zone of Area C (its Israeli military name), where a little boy called Abbas posed for me with an old gas mask on his head. It was most likely left over from one of the riots that regularly flare up during the land disputes in the West Bank.

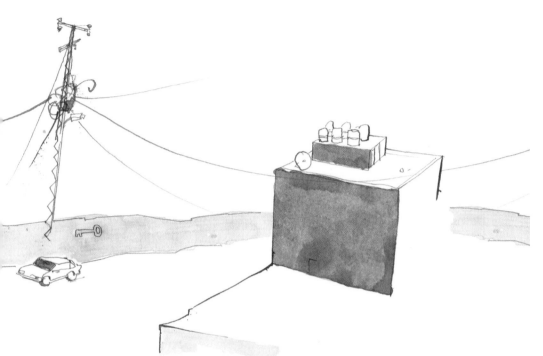

Abbas was a Bedouin, part of an ancient group of people who had moved all across this land with their animals for thousands of years. This kind of migration is harder for them now, as walls and roads have been built across the land. I spoke to Eyad, another Bedouin in Area C, who described the problems they faced. "We used to live in Hebron, but as sheep owners we move from place to place looking for water. I have five brothers and four children, we sell milk and cheese and lamb." Like many Bedouin, and many Palestinians in the West Bank, Eyad is no longer free to move around. Now stationary for the first time in his life, he has built a house for his family, but the land is disputed and the house is under a demolition order. He told me, "They [the Israeli authorities] could come at any time but we have nowhere to go and nothing to do."

In Bethlehem, which is also in the West Bank, I walked along one side of the wall built here by Israel. It was covered in graffiti documenting the war and with messages of love and hate. A man showed me to his rooftop and pointed out his aunt's home on the other side – only a hundred metres away but now separated by an impassable barrier. It wasn't until I had seen these restrictions in Palestine that I appreciated the anxiety caused by taking away people's ability to move.

Iraq

RETURNING HOME

I returned to Mosul in 2018. It was my second visit to Iraq and came a year after Daesh (ISIS) had been defeated there. I wanted to record the Iraqis rebuilding their homes after the end of the occupation. The city had been under Daesh rule for three years and had been the scene of fierce fighting for much of that time. Many people had continued to live here under Daesh, but had had to leave for camps or relatives' homes when the final offensive by the Iraqi Army began in 2016. Now, they were returning home to West Mosul for the first time.

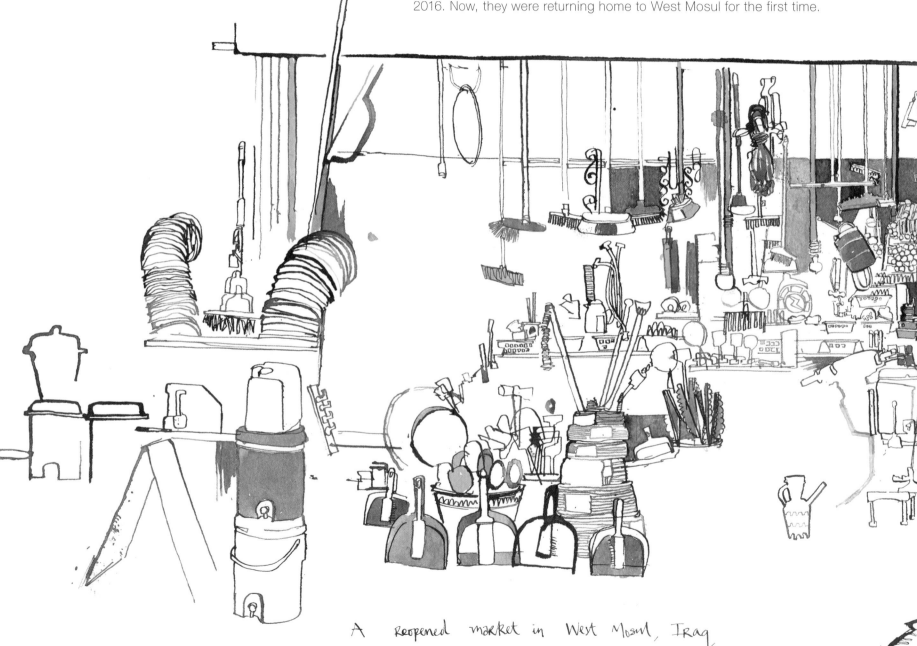

A reopened market in West Mosul, Iraq

When I arrived, only one of the five bridges connecting East and West Mosul, which had been blown up by Daesh as they retreated, had been repaired. Traffic trickled through, bringing back some basic services, workers, the occasional family and a glimmer of hope that normal life could be resumed. I stopped to draw a market that was coming back to life, with stallholders setting out their products. Almost all the people I had met who had fled war wanted to return home. Humans are endlessly resilient and able to pick up where they left off.

Over the course of my weeks in Mosul I often ate in a local falafel shop. One day Muhammad, the owner, asked if I wanted to see what had happened to his home. He had moved his family to the east of the city just before it was hit in an air strike. When I asked Muhammad what belongings he had left, he looked me in the eye to make sure I understood what he was about to say. "Nothing… Nothing… Nothing," he repeated. I found this difficult to imagine until I saw the empty, charred shell of his living room – paint burnt off the walls and unrecognizable plastic things melted in the dust.

Another day I visited the largely abandoned old souk (marketplace) in the centre of the town. A couple of store-owners sat for me to draw them. One man, Zouhair, looked over my shoulder whilst I drew. When I turned my attention to him he initially posed, but as time went on he relaxed and laughed with his friends who had gathered behind me. He told me, "I was one of the first to reopen my shop in the souk. I have worked here for fifty-three years, since I was five I worked in this shop. I have only missed eighteen months whilst the bridges were closed during the fighting."

Zouhair

The bomb-damaged al-Nuri mosque.

Exploring the old city, I walked towards the site of the famous al-Nuri mosque. It wasn't difficult to find people to talk to who had returned home. They were easy to spot, often in the only house on a street with signs of life, with water splashed on the road or an empty chair waiting for the shade to come round.

I sat to draw Yusef Fateh, whose home had once sat at the bottom of the mosque minaret. Yusef told me, "In April 2015 I was accused by Daesh of smuggling people out of West Mosul, which I admitted. I was blindfolded and spent eighteen days in a Daesh prison. I was thrashed 300 times." He showed me a tattered copy of his Daesh court paper. "They released me at 11 a.m. on a Friday. They threw me onto the street and said, 'If you look round we will kill you directly.' At 12 p.m. I packed and left for Syria without my family."

Yusef returned in October 2017 to find his home destroyed by Daesh, along with the al-Nuri mosque. He told me he can't find work because of the wounds on his back, but like many others sees this place as his home. For the time being that is enough for him.

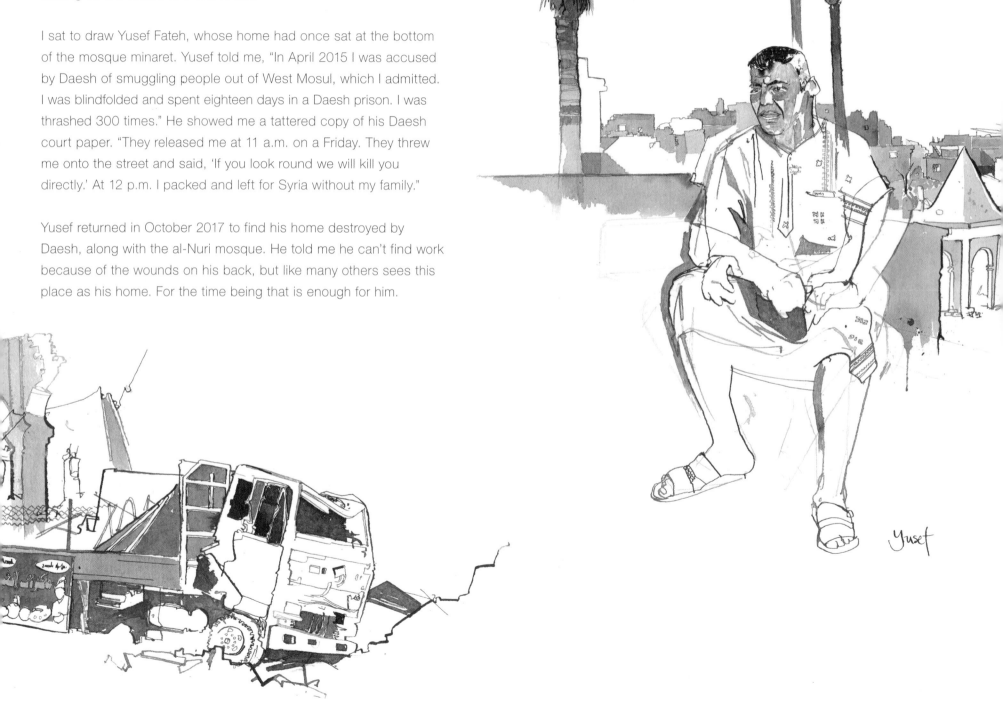

Yusef

Lebanon

LEAVING EVERYTHING BEHIND

In 2011 I drove east from Beirut, the capital of Lebanon, into the Bekaa Valley, accompanying a small humanitarian team working for Doctors of the World. I realized how close I was to the Syrian border when I received a text from the Syrian phone network: "Welcome to Syria… If you have any complaints please contact the Ministry of Information." This message felt bizarre given the ongoing crisis in the country.

During the early stages of the Syrian war more than one million Syrians fled to Lebanon, a country with a population of only around five million people. We visited several families living in tents along the border. Lebanon doesn't recognize them as refugees and so by law doesn't have to build camps for them, so many worked on farms in return for space to put up a tent.

These families showed us the belongings they had carried with them from their homes. They were the belongings of people who had not planned to leave Syria. They were the items they picked up in a rush, or as the lights went out, the items that were left in the rubble of their homes or that they had in their cars when they abandoned them at the border. These were people who thought they would be going home very soon.

As her children, Maram and Hassan, laid their possessions out on the floor in front of me, Rawaa described the moment when they left their home in Homs behind. "I packed the whole box from the kitchen because it was easier than looking for the torch. The children picked their toys. Hassan picked the scary troll. We had to spend one night in the mountains before we arrived here."

Rania's doll

When they arrived in Lebanon they found the box also contained batteries, broken lighters and a TV remote – all useless, but now the only connection they had with their home. These once ordinary belongings now carried huge emotions with them.

I drew the doll of a little Palestinian girl who had fled Syria, called Rania. She watched me and asked if the unfinished drawing had no legs because the doll had lost them in the war. I realized the things that children learn to consider ordinary in war are sometimes the most terrifying to witness.

Some people had left more than belongings behind. Hassan, from Qatana in Syria, showed me a passport photo of his seven-year-old son, Muhammad, who he had left behind in Syria with his grandparents so that he could continue with school. The photo was all he had.

The belongings carried by Rawaa's family from Syria.

Iraqi Kurdistan

NEW HOMES

In 2014 thousands of Yazidi people fled Daesh (ISIS) in Iraq across the mountains around Sinjar, in the north of the country. One of the places they settled was at Khanke, near Duhok in Iraqi Kurdistan. I visited them in 2018 to see the new homes they had made there.

I met Mustafa, who had fled here with his entire family in a Toyota car, all sixteen of them and their belongings. The car was now broken and useless but they kept it, parked outside their new home. It was an emblem of what they had been through. As we walked through his new neighbourhood Mustafa told me his story.

"In the early morning of 3rd August 2014 … we heard that ISIS attacked the Yazidis … we decided to drive to Duhok Province. The whole way there we saw hundreds of people running and walking toward [the] Sinjar mountains – because they didn't have vehicles and at the same time the main road was so crowded with all types of vehicles. At the beginning we were thinking we would go back soon … but after we heard that thousands of Yazidis got killed by ISIS… it's become impossible even to think to go back home. We realized we should find a new place to live in."

Tarpaulin had been wrapped around wooden frames to make accommodation for the Yazidi families. Although the tents were fragile there were signs of permanence: sunflowers grew, toys lay in the dust, a tiny lawn had been seeded and a corrugated fence marked each plot on the land beside the main road.

Jeelan

A Yazidi temporary settlement near Duhok Iraqi. Kurdistan

White rabbits swarmed around, chased by a mob of children. The kids brought me a plastic chair and I drew a young girl called Jeelan. She eventually caught a rabbit and picked it up by its ears, something she had obviously seen an adult do, and which suggested these rabbits were not pets.

I'll never forget Jeelan's infectious smile. It reminded me that a home can be made anywhere – even if it's temporary.

Endings . . . .

The people in this book shaped my view of the world more than I could ever have realized when I sat down to draw them. I'm often asked how people react when I approach them, and the answer is always with politeness and generosity.

I came across many different ways in which migrants and refugees were treated and found it difficult to reconcile the different stories I heard. I saw desperate migrants stuck behind fences in Europe whilst others were welcomed with open arms into homes elsewhere. The process of making this book quickly confirmed that there are many unresolved issues as to how we respond to migration.

The end of this book is not the end of the stories of the people in it. I realize now that this was a small moment in their lives, and whilst meeting them was significant to me it was probably not to them. A drawing is not like a photograph – it's not just about recording something, it can hold huge meaning too. Whatever others make of them, these drawings and the people they represent mean everything to me.

Mama Nazak is now living in Istanbul, and is sad she can't return to Syria or treat her sons' war wounds. Abdullo was deported from Russia after one year and is now back in Tajikistan with his family. Ezat made it out of Belgrade and now lives in Toulouse. Mustafa remains in Duhok but his mother and father sought asylum in Germany. Bassam, who lost his leg in 2013, would be eighteen this year, but sadly we have lost touch. Where will they all be in another ten years?

For many people, perhaps even some of you reading this book, the idea of migrating is an alien one. The faces I sat and drew for hours and hours that fill these pages tell a different story. For them migration is not usually a first choice, but it is more common. Neither innately good or inherently bad, it is just a part of life – the right to move for a better future.

Farbie

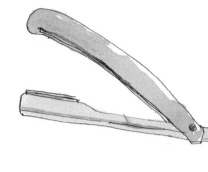

Ideal Net

DINGLING

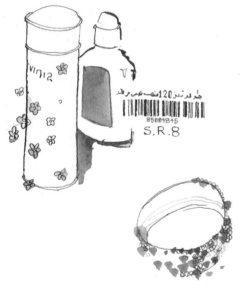

sinia

S.R.8

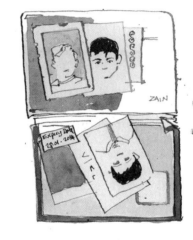

ZAIN

Expiry Date
29.01.2014